Successful
Business Plans
in a week

IAIN MAITLAND

Hodder & Stoughton

A MEMBER OF THE HODDER HEADLINE GROUP

Orders: please contact Bookpoint Ltd, 39 Milton Park, Abingdon, Oxon OX14 4TD. Telephone: (44) 01235 400414, Fax: (44) 01235 400454. Lines are open from 9.00 - 6.00, Monday to Saturday, with a 24 message answering service. Email address: orders@bookpoint.co.uk

British Library Cataloguing in Publication Data
A catalogue record for this title is available from the British Library

ISBN 0 340 71199 X

First published 1996
Second edition 1998

Impression number	10	9	8	7	6	5	4	3
Year			2002		2001		2000	1999

Typeset by Multiplex Techniques Ltd, St Mary Cray, Kent.
Printed in Great Britain for Hodder & Stoughton Educational, a division of Hodder Headline Plc, 338 Euston Road, London NW1 3BH by Cox and Wyman Ltd., Reading, Berkshire.

the Institute of Management

F O U N D A T I O N

The mission of the Institute of Management (IM) is to promote the art and science of management.

The Institute embraces all levels of management from student to chief executive and supports its own Foundation which provides a unique portfolio of services for all managers, enabling them to develop skills and achieve management excellence.

For information on the various levels and benefits of membership, please contact:

Department HS
Institute of Management
Cottingham Road
Corby
Northants NN17 1TT
Tel: 01536 204222
Fax: 01536 201651

This series is commissioned by the Institute of Management Foundation.

■■■■■ C O N T E N T S ■■■■■

All businesses should plan ahead, especially when they wish to raise finance, attract investment, encourage assistance or improve their overall performance. They need to know exactly *what* they want, and *when* and *how* they are going to get there – otherwise, they cannot expect to progress, let alone achieve their objectives.

A business plan can help them to do this. It is a document which sets out the activities of a firm and explains how and when its various objectives will be reached. Usually, such a plan consists of a commercial section detailing key aspects of the concern, a financial section outlining money matters, and appendices which substantiate and elaborate on these two sections. In essence, a business plan provides a framework for the firm to work *within* and *towards*.

The aim of this book is to cut through all the theory and waffle that exists about business plans and show you how to write a successful one. We shall look at this core skill on a clear, step-by-step basis, taking one step each day as follows:

Sunday	Understanding business plans
Monday	Making preparatory notes
Tuesday	Composing the commercial section
Wednesday	Compiling the financial section
Thursday	Adding the appendices
Friday	Submitting a business plan
Saturday	Presenting a business plan

Understanding business plans

Today, we will take a broad, introductory look at business plans. We need to understand what makes them successful before we can go on to write one over the rest of the week. In particular, we should consider their:

- contents
- uses
- key features

Contents

Not surprisingly, all business plans are different, but most
of them will contain three main sections:

- a commercial section
- a financial section
- appendices

A commercial section
In this first section, we would normally include some
preliminary materials such as a title page, contents page
and introduction. These would then be followed by text
about our business, products and services, team, market
and overall objectives. The names and order of these
subjects and the precise information given about them may
vary from one plan to another, but they should *all* be
covered in some detail somewhere in this section.

A financial section
Equally important, if not more so in some instances, the
financial section of a business plan will usually incorporate
a profit budget and cash-flow forecast indicating the
estimated profits and ongoing cash position within the firm
over a given period of time. These will often be
accompanied by past or projected – or both – annual
accounts, such as a profit and loss account and a balance
sheet, plus details of current financial circumstances and
requirements.

Appendices
This final section comprises photographs, samples, letters,
forms, documents and other items of independent origin

which verify and occasionally add to all of the statements, financial facts and figures laid down in the commercial and financial sections. In many respects, these appendices can be viewed as the foundation of a successful business plan: without them, the preceding text is simply a mass of unsubstantiated opinions and hearsay.

Here is a checklist of what we might include in our business plan:

1 Commercial section:

- title page
- contents page
- introduction
- the business
- products and services
- the team
- the market
- objectives

2 Financial section:

- profit budget
- cash-flow forecast
- past accounts
- future accounts
- current financial circumstances
- financial requirements

3 Appendices:

- photographs
- samples
- letters
- forms
- documents
- other items

Uses

We may compile a business plan for various reasons. Most often, it will be used to:

- raise finance
- attract investment
- encourage assistance
- improve performance

Raise finance
If we need funds to start, buy or expand a firm in some way, a plan may be sent to a prospective lender such as a bank or building society manager, charitable trust, venture capital house or even family or friends who have savings or redundancy money available. Hopefully, we can convince the relevant parties both that we have a viable proposal *and* that we will be able to make capital and interest payments on time.

Attract investment
Similarly, the business plan could be used to attract investment, and would in this case be written to highlight the firm's forthcoming activities and potential profits, and

the possible risks and returns for would-be investors. Such a plan may be forwarded to wealthy individuals and to organisations like venture capital institutions which specialise in investing in up-and-coming companies, especially those trading in new and innovative activities.

Encourage assistance
Sometimes, we need help from other people and organisations in order to trade successfully and prosper. Perhaps we want a prospective landlord to grant a lease to us, a supplier to enter into a sole agency agreement for our town, or a fellow trader to allow us to use their storage and distribution facilities. These parties may be more willing to do what we want if they have been given a plan which outlines both our requirements and intentions *and* the mutual benefits arising from them.

Improve performance
Even if we do not require external finance, investment or assistance, it is still a good idea to draw up a business plan anyway, for our own internal use. Preparing commercial and financial sections (and appendices where appropriate) enables us to assess our business in an objective manner. We may get to know it better, along with its individual strengths and weaknesses, and be able to set more realistic objectives as a consequence of this increased knowledge and understanding.

Just as significantly, a business plan provides us with a commercial and financial framework against which we can regularly compare our performance to see if we are on course to achieve our objectives. Possible problems such as rising costs and imminent cash shortfalls can hopefully be spotted and resolved well in advance. If reviewed and amended at monthly intervals, our plan enables us to monitor, control and improve the overall performance of our business – perhaps this is the most important function of a business plan.

Key features

So, we know what a business plan is, what it contains and how we can use it. We now need to think about those key features that distinguish a successful business plan from an unsuccessful one. Obviously, we will wish to incorporate these into the plan that we are going to write.

Ideally, our business plan will be:

- well researched
- adapted
- attractive
- understandable
- realistic
- well supported

Well researched

A successful business plan is researched fully, and is only completed once all the commercial, financial and supporting information that may need to be included in it has been gathered together. The plan should create the impression that the writer knows everything there is to know and can prove it. As soon as the reader thinks of something they wish to see, they should be able to find it. And if they want proof of a statement, it should be readily available in the appendices.

Adapted

Of course, not *all* of the facts and figures that we are going to collect should be put into the plan – otherwise it might run to tens or even hundreds of pages! Its content, structure, emphasis and length must vary according to what our particular reader wants to know about and how much time they have to read it. For example, a bank manager wishes to know about commercial activities but only in relation to likely profits, cash flow and financial requirements. A prospective landlord, on the other hand, may want to learn about how our business and activities might affect other tenants, but little else. However much information we want to incorporate – and there is no right or wrong length for a business plan – we must try to keep it as brief and to the point as we can. Always asking 'Is this relevant?' before noting anything down should help us to achieve this. The reader will only have a certain amount of time to study our plan, and needs to be able to do it swiftly. We can assist them in doing this by omitting irrelevant, superfluous and repetitive material.

Attractive
A winning business plan must have a smart and professional appearance, especially if it is being sent out to raise finance, attract investment or encourage assistance in some way. This will give the writer an efficient, businesslike image and should put the reader in a more

favourable mood towards both them and any proposition that they are making. Clearly, the business proposal itself must still be a viable one if it is to be accepted, but it obviously helps to get the reader on our side as far as possible.

Our business plan must be put inside a clean and classy file or folder: this not only creates a professional impression but also protects the material from becoming torn and dirty as it is being passed around. We should choose a file which matches our image – colourful and jazzy if we are artistic, plain and dark if we are methodical and serious. For easy identification, it is a good idea to place a white sticker on the front of the file and type (or write neatly) the title of the plan on it along with our name, address, 'phone/fax number and the date. A business logo adds a classy touch too:

 KALEIDOSCOPE
A
BUSINESS PROPOSAL
BY
TOM HUDSON
2, THE COTTAGES, NEWTOWN, SUFFOLK FE7 3BH
TEL/FAX: 01394 770512 DATE: 1 MAY 1998

To emphasise our professionalism, we need to use top-quality, A4 paper, perhaps selecting white or another shade if we want to coordinate colours to achieve a particular style and image. The text should be typed, rather than handwritten and amateurish, and should be set out carefully. We ought to include generous margins at the top, sides and bottom of each page, plenty of headings and subheadings, short paragraphs of similar length, and bullet points where appropriate. These all help to improve the overall appearance, making it easier to read, and give the reader sufficient room in which to note comments and queries.

Here is an example of what we should be aiming for:

About Kaleidoscope

- *Its purpose*
  Kaleidoscope is being set up in order to meet the needs of those families who wish to hire rather than buy nursery goods and equipment, typically overnight and on an occasional basis
- *Its location*
  It will be based in a newly built, 500-square-metre showroom alongside of our home. This is within two minutes' walking distance of the town's only health centre, St John's Playgroup and Newtown Primary School (see 'Appendix 2: Newtown Map' on pages 3–4 of the appendices)
- *Its products and services*
  Initially, we will stock the following goods:
  - Moses baskets
  - carrycots
  - cribs
  - baby bouncers
  - baby walkers
  - highchairs

We should always submit top copies of typed sheets, rather than photocopies which would create the impression that this is little more than a circular being sent out to everyone. (We can, however, put extra, clean copies of the plan at the back of our file or folder if we know that several people will wish to study it.) The text must be free from any spelling mistakes, typing errors or inaccuracies such as incorrectly added figures. These will confuse and muddle the reader and damage our reputation. We need to check, check *and* check again – and then retype, if necessary.

Understandable
Our language must match the reader's knowledge and understanding of the subject matter. We should use clear, simple words and phrases when addressing a layperson who may be bewildered by trade jargon. Likewise, we should incorporate technical expressions where appropriate when writing to an expert who might otherwise feel patronised. The key to success here is to think carefully about what our reader knows, and to pitch our language at the right level. It is important that we never automatically assume they are as familiar with the subject as we are – this is rarely the case.

Whatever we have to say, we must ensure that we use *specific* words and phrases, rather than vague ones such as 'good', 'nice', 'better than' and 'cheaper than' which will be defined differently by each reader. For example, '£33.95' is understood clearly, whereas 'a good price' means nothing. Humorous comments and statements must be avoided at all times too. What *we* find funny may be interpreted in another way by a person with an alternative sense of humour. Our joke could be seen as flippant and, when finance or investment is being sought, humour is often considered to be inappropriate.

Realistic

Obviously, we need to sound 100 per cent confident and enthusiastic about our firm and its prospects – after all, if we are not, we cannot expect the reader to be either! Nevertheless, we must not get too carried away, as this may make us sound foolish and could undermine what we are stating. Most readers will possess some knowledge of what we are writing about, and will be able to distinguish between facts and fantasy.

Our statements and financial figures need to be sensible and achievable. We should base them on solid, reliable evidence such as past income and expenditure and definite sales orders. Prospective difficulties must be addressed fully rather than being glossed over or ignored completely. We should identify and then explain clearly how we are going to overcome, or at least cope with, them. By not referring to them, we simply appear evasive or incompetent. It is sensible to deal in detail only with the immediate future, namely the coming year: the longer ahead we look, the more speculative our comments become. Our reader is more interested in reality than hopes and dreams.

Well supported

A successful business plan always backs up its commercial and financial sections with independent evidence in its appendices. Our comments alone will not be accepted at face value, especially if large sums of money are involved. We therefore have to be willing *and* able to prove everything we say is true by supplying additional, verifying material from reputable sources, and ideally, independent ones.

Summary

To sum up what we have learned today:

- A business plan usually contains:
  - a commercial section
  - a financial section
  - appendices

- It can be used to:
  - raise finance
  - attract investment
  - encourage assistance
  - improve performance

- A successful business plan is:
  - well researched
  - adapted
  - attractive
  - understandable
  - realistic
  - supported

Making preparatory notes

Following Sunday's work, we know what we are aiming
for. The next step is to draw up some detailed, preparatory
notes for our own successful business plan. This means:

- conducting internal research
- using external sources
- accumulating appropriate information

Conducting internal research

Much of the information we need to put into our business
plan can be obtained relatively easily, from in-house
sources:

- our own knowledge
- our colleagues
- books and records

Our own knowledge
More often than not, our understanding of the business will be greater than anyone else's. We may have established the firm and perhaps now sell the goods, recruit the team, deal personally with customers, and so on. Who else knows as much as us? Probably nobody! We should therefore draw upon our own background knowledge and information before proceeding further.

Possibly the best way of doing this is to ask ourselves lots of questions to see if we can answer them. Here are some to start us off:

- What is our business?
- What does it do?
- Whereabouts is it located?
- What are the premises like?
- What equipment, machinery and vehicles do we have?
- What do we sell?
- What are our products and services like?
- What are our rivals' goods and services like?
- Who works for the firm?
- What are their backgrounds?
- What do they do?
- What are their strengths and weaknesses?
- Who are our customers?
- How much do we know about them?
- Who are our competitors?
- What do we know about them?
- What is the marketplace like?
- How much do we know about it?
- What are our personal goals?
- What are our business objectives?
- How have we been doing financially?
- What are our finances like now?
- What will our finances be like in the future?
- What cash will be available?
- What profits will we make in the future?
- How can we prove what we know?

Our colleagues

In a larger business with various departments for purchasing, production, marketing, administration, personnel and so forth, some of the data required for the plan may have to be obtained by approaching our work colleagues. Whoever we talk to, we do need to be able to distinguish between opinions and facts. Generally, facts are better than opinions, unless the latter come from independent, reputable sources – which our colleagues are not!

Books and records
Whatever the size of our firm, the books and records that we have accumulated so far will be invaluable to us when we are composing our business plan. In particular, we will find it helpful to refer to previous annual accounts, purchase agreements, sales records and orders, and the like. Details can be taken from these and discussed in the text of the plan, with key documents being placed in the appendices for verification.

Normally, most of the facts that we need for the commercial and financial sections of our business plan will be available in-house. However, we need to remember that everything we write about has to be proved, and this means obtaining supporting data from outside the firm. Our word alone is not enough: other people's carry more weight.

Using external sources

There are many external sources of information and advice available to us. We should consider all of them, and then approach those which are most likely to be of assistance. The following are usually worth contacting:

- banks/building societies
- customers
- suppliers
- competitors
- accountants
- solicitors
- agents
- associations
- government
- media

Banks/building societies

As our bank manager is probably going to receive our plan, it is sensible to get in touch with them beforehand to find out exactly what they want from us. The majority of banks and building societies provide ready-made business plan, profit budget and cash-flow forecast forms for us to complete, and can supply guidance on how to fill these in correctly. Pamphlets and booklets on general business issues and specific details on financial matters are available too. These all make useful background reading.

Customers

Those people and firms who buy our goods and services are an excellent source of advice. They can tell us all we need to know – and to write – about them, including their location, characteristics, wants and needs. In addition, they can give us opinions about our concern and our goods and services which may be useful additions to our appendices. Their comments about our rivals might be revealing as well.

Suppliers

Our suppliers will obviously be able to provide facts and figures about the raw materials, component parts and stocks that we are purchasing from them, along with further, helpful information about mutual customers, competitors and the marketplace. Although some of their additional comments may be biased, these will usually contain one or two points of use to us.

Competitors

Many small businesses compete amicably against each other, with the overall aim of surviving against larger companies trading nearby. If we can establish friendly relationships, we may be able to draw on their knowledge of goods, services, customers and the market. Clearly, we may find out more about *them* as well, which will enable us to then write about them with greater accuracy.

Accountants

Costly though they are, an accountant can put us in touch with potential financiers, provide advice on all money matters, help us to write our financial section, and give our business plan a greater veneer of respectability. It is usually wise to choose an accountant on the basis of recommendations from fellow traders we can trust. We need to be aware of the likely costs involved in using them, and evaluate these alongside of the possible benefits.

Solicitors

We could approach a solicitor for guidance on legal issues that we need to refer to in our plan – partnership agreements, contracts of sale, freehold deeds, leasehold agreements and planning permission, amongst other items. As with an accountant, we should make our choice from personal recommendations and compare the expense against the advantages of referring to them. Evidently, they are invaluable in some instances.

Agents

Business transfer agents who specialise in selling going concerns will be able to supply data about businesses for sale, what to look for and how to value them, as well as information about freehold and leasehold properties, and how to agree rents – all potential text or appendices material for us. Similarly, estate agents can comment on freehold and leasehold premises, prices, rents and rates in our region which may be of some value to our business plan.

Associations

Local chambers of commerce or trade run by business people in the community can be a good source of off-the-record advice about what is happening in the area. Representative associations in our trade or industry can provide or verify much of the commercial information needed. Membership of a nationwide, small-business association confers many benefits for members, including an advisory service on most business issues.

Government

Our local council can be a helpful source of information on such subjects as low-cost finance and grants available, planning-permission procedures and forthcoming developments. Some councils even employ small-business advisers who can assist in the writing of business plans. A variety of statistics, surveys and reports are continually being produced by national government and supplied through its departments such as the Department of Trade and Industry. Many of these contain useful background details for our plan.

Media

Newspapers and magazines may have included articles about our business, products, services, employees, customers and competitors at some time in the past. We may find it beneficial to refer to these once more when compiling our commercial section in particular. Copies of recent articles could then be placed within the appendices to support any comments made.

Here are some other sources of potential use to us:

- architects
- surveyors
- illustrators
- photographers
- printers
- insurance brokers
- libraries
- market research companies

Accumulating appropriate information

We now need to start sorting through the mass of information that has come to us from all the different sources, making notes which subsequently can form the basis of our business plan. We could use these headings:

- The business
- Products and services
- The team
- The market
- Objectives
- Finance
- Appendices

The business

Under this heading, we could jot down notes about our firm or business idea, including whatever we think is most relevant in our situation. Typically, we might write about its history, activities and current position, location and premises, equipment, machinery and vehicles. It is up to us to decide what our reader wants to see.

Products and services

Here, we might note down information about the numbers and types of products and services that we offer, along with their main features and selling points. It is important to make notes too about rival goods and services, comparing and contrasting these with our own. We need to be especially realistic at this point, being aware of our shortcomings and how we are going to deal with them.

The team

Beneath this heading, we should focus on ourselves as well as our colleagues and employees, as appropriate. In particular, we should note our individual careers to date, skills, knowledge, experiences, strengths and weaknesses, and how we all fit together to form a good team.

The market

Here, we should concentrate on our customers – their numbers, types, locations and purchasing habits. We need to make notes about our competitors too – numbers, types, locations, activities, strengths and weaknesses. We could also take a broader look at the marketplace itself, especially its size, changes and developments taking place, and future prospects.

Objectives

It is a good idea for us to write out our personal and business objectives for the short, medium and long term – for the next year, three years and thereafter. We must be cautious, though: a lender will want to see that we are not being overoptimistic and therefore unrealistic.

Finance
If we are planning to include a financial section for a bank manager, or whomever, we should sketch out some preliminary notes about our finances to date, likely future sales, costs and profits, and possible forthcoming cash flow into and out of our account, as well as our current financial circumstances and requirements. If we are trying to raise finance, these notes are essential – indeed, as important as all of the other notes put together.

Appendices
Below this final heading, we should make a note of those items which we can put in to back up our statements. Here is a list of what we might decide to include:

- press cuttings
- map
- property particulars
- photographs of equipment
- product samples
- suppliers' price lists
- our price lists
- sales literature
- competitors' price lists
- competitors' sales literature
- curricula vitae
- certificates/diplomas
- partnership-agreement documents
- company-formation documents
- sales records
- sales orders
- quotes/estimates of costs
- annual accounts
- proof of security
- accountant's/solicitor's comments

Of course, this does not mean we have to include all of these items – we should consider them all carefully, and then select the relevant ones.

Summary

During Monday, we have carried out the following, important tasks:

- conducted internal research, drawing on our own knowledge, and referring to colleagues, books and records too
- used external sources to verify and enhance the information we have gathered together
- accumulated appropriate information about the business, products and services, team, market, objectives and finance, as well as appropriate information for the appendices

Composing the commercial section

Having completed our preparatory work, we can now
move on to make a start on the plan itself – by writing that
all-important commercial section. Today, therefore, we will
consider:

- the preliminaries
- our business
- the products and services
- our team
- the market
- our objectives

The preliminaries

The commercial section should begin with:

* a title page
* a contents page
* an introduction

A title page

This should simply repeat the information given on the file or folder in which the business plan is being submitted. Restating its title plus our name, address, telephone/fax number and the date of compilation will ensure that the plan is instantly recognisable if it is separated from its file.

A contents page

Whoever is studying our business plan will wish to be able to find relevant topics promptly. Thus, a precise and accurate list of contents must be included showing the order of the various subjects we have dealt with and the respective pages to be referred to. We need to draft the contents page and number all of the pages *after* we have completed the entire plan. If we do it any earlier, we will then inevitably think of two or three other items which need to be put somewhere in the text. Renumbered pages – with '11a' and '11b' slotted in and '12' rewritten as '13' and so on – look sloppy and convey a slapdash image. We must avoid this at all costs.

An introduction

We should never underestimate the significance of an introduction: it can mean the difference between success and failure. Bankers, prospective investors and other interested parties will probably be busy, with little time to study every business plan sent to them. Their initial impression of our plan therefore will decide whether it receives either their full, undivided attention or no more than a cursory glance before rejection.

To convince the recipient that our plan deserves to be studied, we should broadly summarise the text. We might say what our business is selling, who our customers are and what objectives we have. Most important of all to the reader, we must then explain *what it is* that we want them to do for us – provide finance, supply goods or whatever. Ideally, we will also point out *what is in it for them* if they do help us – after all, *that*, more than anything else, is going to persuade them to read on!

As with the contents page, we should write the introduction once we have finished the rest of the plan – otherwise we will only have to redo it if we subsequently decide to change the order of the subjects. Looking at each section in turn, 'Our business', 'Products and services' and so forth, we should sum them up in one or two sentences. If these are all then put together and trimmed to remove vague and repetitive comments, we should have a first-rate introduction which is both brief *and* informative.

Our business

With our earlier notes to hand, we can start writing about the business, in particular:

- its background
- its location
- its premises

Its background

If the business has been trading for some time, we should set out its track record to date – when, where and why it was launched, how it has progressed to reach its current position, its achievements and the obstacles overcome. If we are buying a business, we should say why it is for sale – and the reason should be the *real* one, which may not necessarily be the same as that given by the vendor! On the other hand, we could be getting ready to start a business from scratch. If so, we must supply background information about our ideas instead – what made us think of this business, why we believe it will be successful, how, where and when we will start trading. Everything we write down should be supported by substantiating evidence – balance sheets, profit and loss accounts, a business transfer agent's details, an accountant's letter, newspaper and magazine clippings and the like.

Its location

We should write about the location too – the reasons for basing the business there, its advantages, and its disadvantages and how we are working to overcome them. We must also mention any anticipated changes taking place in the locality, such as a new factory or road, and state how we will deal with the opportunities and challenges that arise as a result.

An excellent way of supporting this text is to slot a map into the appendices. On this, we should highlight the positions of our business, suppliers, customers, competitors and other key data such as influential neighbours and any attractions which draw people into the area, like free car parks. Sometimes, it can be helpful to include two maps, one a close-up of the firm and its immediate vicinity, the other a map of the town or trading region.

Its premises

If we are buying a property, we should note the asking price, the amount of capital we have to invest, why we want to buy instead of rent and what we will do if the business fails. We must be realistic here. If we are renting, we should refer to any premium we will have to pay, the amount and frequency of rental payments, service charges and the date of the next rent review. Again, we must say what we will do with the lease if the business is unsuccessful.

Next, we should specify the dimensions of our premises and the internal and external layouts, plus the equipment, machinery and vehicles used. We need to explain whether these are owned or leased, how long they will last for, when we will need to replace them and what they *are* and *will be* worth.

Again, it is essential that we substantiate everything we have stated to prove it is all true. We might think about putting in the estate agent's particulars, a copy of the freehold deeds or leasehold agreement, the solicitor's and surveyor's reports, and photographs and diagrams of equipment, machinery and vehicles, as appropriate.

The products and services

Going on with this section, we should concentrate on
detailing our products and services as appropriate – more
specifically:

- their main features
- their unique selling points

Their main features
We must state what our products and services are and how
they contribute towards our stock and sales levels. We
should outline what these products look like, how they
work and what they can be used for. With services, we
must state what they involve us doing for customers. It
may be a good idea to explain how we make or buy our
goods – production processes, output and quality control,
suppliers, terms and conditions of sale.

We should also mention our prices plus any discounts
offered for bulk buys or prompt payments, saying why
goods and services are priced at that level, and showing
them to be competitively priced *and* profitable. It is
important to write about advertising and selling methods
too – how we advertise and sell our products and services,
why our choices are effective, who sells our goods, how
they are distributed, and so on.

We then have to decide what verifying documents should
be included in the appendices. It is useful to put in
photographs, illustrations and newspaper cuttings – even
samples of our goods, if there is room for them. As

relevant, we could also include production schedules, suppliers' price lists, letters or invoices stating costs, our price guide and advertising and promotional materials.

Their unique selling points
If our products and services are to sell, they must have some obvious advantages over competing goods. Thus, we should provide a short list of our main rivals, with brief descriptions of each of them. We need to put the same type of information about our rivals into the appendices as we did for our own products and services – photos, price lists and sales and advertising literature are a must. Adding samples is a sound idea as well.

It is important to highlight the advantages that our goods have over competing ones *and* how these will be maintained. Being realistic, we must also refer to any disadvantages that our products and services may have, explaining how we intend to remedy them. A timetable showing when the changes and improvements will be made may be a useful addition to the business plan.

Our team

When composing the commercial section, we must never forget to detail the most important ingredient of any business: the people within it – that means us! Therefore, we should make sure that we include one or two paragraphs about:

- ourselves
- colleagues and employees

Ourselves

It is often said that most financiers and investors are primarily backing the *people* involved, with money and assistance being provided on the strength of their personalities, skills, knowledge, experiences and finances. Every statement we make about ourselves must indicate that we have what it takes to be successful!

It is probably best to approach this part of the text in a chronological order, working forward from our school or college days through our career or business history up to the present time. We need to verify our comments with a curriculum vitae, photocopies of certificates and diplomas, press cuttings and even congratulatory letters about our work from former employers or satisfied customers. Let's not hide our light under a bushel!

Colleagues and employees

We should describe our business colleagues in the same way that we wrote about ourselves, outlining their careers to date, drawing in personalities, skills and so forth, and saying what they'll be doing for the firm. If we are jointly controlling a business, it is sensible to discuss the key points of our partnership agreement, how much capital is being introduced by each person, the salaries to be paid, how profits and losses will be shared out, the length of the partnership and how it can be dissolved.

We can then refer to our key employees, such as managers, detailing their past and present jobs plus future roles in the business. After this, we could list the remaining employees, perhaps by name, job title and duties. If there are many of them, it is wiser to state the numbers employed in each department instead. We must not forget to mention the wages we pay to them, either per employee or per department. If we have to buy in any services that cannot be done in-house, we should refer to these here as well, along with a note of the expenses involved.

Relevant documents for our appendices would include curricula vitae of key personnel, copies of certificates and diplomas, partnership agreements and company-formation documents plus written estimates of likely professional fees – in short, anything that will back up what we have just put down in writing.

The market

Ever conscious of our preparatory notes, we can press ahead and write about the marketplace, and most notably:

* the customers
* the competitors

The customers
If there are not too many of them, we should supply key customers' names and addresses here *or* in the appendices, as appropriate. Alternatively, we can identify them in terms of sex, age, income and occupation (or a combination of these). It is sensible to say how many there are, where they are located and how much, and when and why, they will buy from us. We can then discuss the market as a whole plus our share of this. It is advisable to explain how these circumstances may change in the future, and how we will deal with these developments.

We should substantiate the comments we have made about our customers by incorporating documents such as sales records, orders and a map showing where they are. It is wise to support our statements about the market by obtaining matching assessments from reliable, independent sources: chambers of commerce, trade associations and the like.

The competitors

We ought to supply a thumbnail sketch of each competitor in terms of their history, activities, location, premises, goods, customers and market share. Being realistic, we need to say how they are better than us and how we intend to cancel out these advantages. Also, we should state how they are less successful than we are and what we are going to do to keep ahead of them.

As always, we have to back our comments with hard evidence. We should slip into the appendices any newspaper cuttings about their recent activities, successes and failures, a map showing where they are based, photographs of their premises, and sales literature too. We must prove that what we have stated is a true and fair assessment and not just our personal, biased opinion.

Our objectives

By now, the recipient knows almost everything about the commercial aspects of our plan. We should conclude this section – and today's work – by referring to our objectives. These can be divided into:

- the short term
- the medium term
- the long term

The short term

We must detail our goals over the coming year, saying what we intend to do to achieve them. Although these will probably be clear in our mind, it can be helpful to read back what we have written so far just to refresh our memory and to prioritise them. Whatever they are, we must make certain that they are realistic and within our capabilities. It is best to err on the side of caution so that we can subsequently impress the reader by surpassing expectations, rather than failing to meet them.

The medium term

It is then a good idea to discuss our objectives for the following two years, stating how we will fulfil these. Talk only in general terms about this period, as it is unlikely we will be able to make any truly accurate predictions this far into the future. After all, if we were asked three years ago to anticipate our progress to date, we probably wouldn't have imagined we'd be where we are now!

The long term
Finally, we need to sketch out our more distant goals, three years on and thereafter. Whatever our hopes – and they cannot be much more than that at this stage – we must make them sound sensible and achievable.

If the reader isn't interested in seeing a financial section – perhaps a would-be landlord just wants to check that our commercial activities won't clash with those of our fellow tenants – then we will conclude the text here. Being concise, we could possibly remind the recipient what it is we want from them, and how this will both help us to reach our objectives and benefit them as well.

Summary

Today, we have discussed what goes into the commercial section of a successful business plan. We have written about:

- the preliminaries, incorporating a title page, contents page and introduction
- our business, most notably its background, location and premises
- the products and services, and their features and main selling points
- our team, including ourselves, our colleagues and our employees
- the market, customers and competitors
- our objectives in the short, medium and long term

Compiling the financial section

On Tuesday, we worked through the commercial section. Now, we turn our attention to the accompanying financial section which will be included in the plan if it is to be used to raise finance, attract investment or monitor financial progress. This section might include:

- a profit budget
- a cash-flow forecast
- annual accounts
- financial requirements

A profit budget

This budget is concerned with how profitably the firm is trading (or not!) – an example of a profit-budget form is shown on page 46. The budget can be broken down into various parts and tackled accordingly:

- sales
- direct costs
- overheads
- profits
- explanatory notes
- supporting documents

Sales

We have already anticipated our sales income for the coming year and commented on it in our commercial section. We should now write out our estimated monthly sales in the budget boxes across the form. It is important that we record these sales when we expect them to be made rather than paid for as we are concentrating here on whether or not the business is making sufficient money. The timings of income and expenditure and their effects on our cash resources are looked at later when we tackle the cash-flow forecast.

Direct costs

Direct – or 'variable' – costs fluctuate directly in line with the number of goods produced and sold: the higher the level of sales, the higher the direct costs – and vice versa! There are two main categories of direct cost: 'materials' covers expenditure on raw materials, component parts, packaging and deliveries, whilst 'wages' refers to the sums paid to production-line workers, sales representatives and the like. We need to note the monthly amounts involved here in the appropriate budget columns. Deducting direct costs from sales leaves us with our 'gross profit'.

Profit-budget form

	Month:		Month:		Month:		Month:		Month:		Month:		Totals	
	Budget	Actual	Budget	Actual	Budget	Actual	Budget	Actual	Budget	Actual	Budget	Actual	Budget	Actual
Sales														
Less: materials														
wages														
Gross profit														
Overheads: salaries														
Rent, rates, water														
Insurance														
Repairs, renewals														
Heat, light, power														
Postage														
Printing, stationery														
Transport														
Telephone														
Professional fees														
Depreciation														
Interest charges														
Other														
Total overheads														
Trading profit														

Overheads

These are those fixed items of expenditure such as rent and
rates which have to be paid come what may, however
many goods are being produced or sold. We need to add
up the estimated annual cost of each category of overhead,
divide the total by 12 and place the resulting monthly
figures in the correct boxes. Remember, we are focusing
here on *profit*, not cash flow. Totting up the various entries
in the monthly columns gives us our 'total overheads'.
Subtracting these from our gross profit leaves us with our
'trading profit'.

Profits

Our gross and trading profit figures are very important to
us. The gross profit figure shows how efficiently we are
buying, manufacturing and selling goods. Our 'gross profit
margin' can be calculated by dividing gross profit by sales
and multiplying by 100. The resulting figure can then be
compared with the trade average, and conclusions can be
drawn about our performance. The trading profit figure, in
turn tells us if the business is truly profitable, and, if so,
whether or not satisfactory levels of profit are being
achieved.

Explanatory notes

The profit budget is only as good as its explanatory notes.
After all, *we* may know why we have included certain
figures, but the bank manager or whoever else is studying
it might not – so we need to tell them! Thus, we should put
'1', '2', '3' next to 'Sales', 'Materials', 'Wages' and so on, and
attach one or two typed A4 sheets which set out each item
on a point-by-point basis and explain how we arrived at

our figures. We have to convince the reader that what
we've put will be correct.

Here is an example of what we could write:

10 Postage

We have budgeted to spend £20 per week on general
correspondence with existing and prospective
customers. This is in line with last year's spending –
see 'Appendix 6, Annual Accounts', pages 13–14.

11 Printing/stationery

Westbridge Printing will supply us with their standard
pack of letterheads, compliment slips, business cards
and envelopes at a cost of £520. Refer to 'Appendix 7,
Miscellaneous Quotes', pages 15–22.

Supporting documents
Wherever possible, figures and explanatory notes must be
backed up by hard, independent evidence. We need to
accumulate items such as sales orders, suppliers' price lists,
estimates and quotations as we go along, referring to them
in our notes and including them in our accompanying
appendices. Ideally, everything we mention here should be
verified in the appendices by another person or
organisation of some standing.

A cash-flow forecast

It is essential that a business not only makes a profit but
always has enough cash reserves available to pay the bills
and keep trading comfortably. A cash-flow forecast shows

how money flows into and out of a firm over a given period of time. An example of a typical form is shown overleaf. The forecast can be viewed in several ways, but the following elements must be involved in its completion:

- receipts
- payments
- balances
- supplementary notes
- back-up materials

Receipts

Incomings will probably derive from three main sources: capital introduced by us, cash from sales made, and cash from debtors (those people or organisations which owe us money). We need to note the relevant amounts in the appropriate budget boxes according to when we expect the money to be *received*. We ought to be rather pessimistic here as it will often be much later than anticipated. Totting up each month's budgeted receipts enables us to complete our 'total receipts' line.

Payments

Most of the relevant information here can be lifted from our profit budget but amended to take account of the timings of outgoings – which will hopefully occur *after* incomings so that a healthy cash flow is maintained at all times. Adding up each month's budgeted payments then allows us to write out the 'total payments' line.

Balances

If we deduct our total monthly receipts from payments, we will be left with our 'net cash flow': and this should be a

Cash-flow forecast

	Month:		Month:		Month:		Month:		Month:		Month:		Totals	
	Budget	Actual	Budget	Actual	Budget	Actual	Budget	Actual	Budget	Actual	Budget	Actual	Budget	Actual
Receipts: capital														
Cash from sales														
Cash from debtors														
Total receipts (A)														
Payments: creditors														
Salaries, wages														
Rent, rates, water														
Insurance														
Repairs, renewals														
Heat, light, power														
Postage														
Printing, stationery														
Transport														
Telephone														
Professional fees														
Capital payments														
Interest charges														
Other														
VAT payable														
Total payments (B)														
Net cash flow (A-B)														
Opening bank balance														
Closing bank balance														

positive rather than a negative sum if we are operating a cash-conscious firm. As relevant, we then add or subtract this amount to or from our 'opening bank balance,' which gives us our 'closing bank balance', for the month. This figure then becomes the opening bank balance for the *next* month, and so on across to the 'totals' column on the right-hand side of the form.

Supplementary notes
All too often, bank managers are sent a highly detailed forecast and are then expected to interpret it correctly without any help. Evidently, this is difficult to do, and will not put the reader in a good mood towards us. As with the profit budget, we should therefore note, '1', '2', '3' and so forth down the side of the form and explain the figures point-by-point on attached A4 sheets of paper.

Back-up materials
Similarly, we need to prove as far as possible that what we have forecasted will actually happen over the coming months. The best way of doing this is to refer to back-up materials, such as loan-agreement forms, letters from debtors and suppliers' terms of sale, and to include these in the appendices. Our own word and opinions are not enough proof: we need to substantiate these with comments and statements from other, independent people and firms.

Annual accounts

Having spent some time calculating our finances over the next year, it is a good idea to look at where we will be

financially at that time. We can do this by drawing up two
statements from the data accumulated so far:

- a profit and loss account
- a balance sheet

A profit and loss account
This financial statement summarises the sales, total costs
and profits or losses of a firm over a specific period of time,
usually one year. This statement is easy to put together
since almost all of the relevant information can be taken
from our profit budget. We must remember, however, to
deal only with *invoiced* income and expenditure here –
when the bills are *actually paid* is disregarded. As
appropriate, one or two explanatory notes may need to be
added for clarification purposes.

Here is an example of a profit and loss account:

Sales		368,327
Opening stock	42,322	
Purchases	127,400	
Closing stock	44,170	
Cost of sales		125,552
Gross profit		242,775

Overheads:

Salaries/wages	67,528	
Rent/rates/water	36,240	
Insurance	5,750	
Repairs/renewals	2,300	
Heat/light/power	1,060	
Postage	1,030	
Printing/stationery	1,260	
Transport	1,241	
Telephone	860	
Depreciation	752	
Total		118,021
Net profit		124,754

A balance sheet
Our second statement shows our firm's assets and liabilities
at a given time and indicates how its activities have been
funded. Normally, a balance sheet will be drawn up at
yearly intervals alongside of a profit and loss account.
Much of the data contained within it can be lifted from our
profit-budget and cash-flow forecast forms. An example of
a balance sheet is shown on page 54.

Fixed assets		159,600
Current assets:		
Stock	32,300	
Debtors	5,750	
Cash	5,620	
	43,670	
Current liabilities:		
Overdraft	2,600	
Creditors	9,720	
	12,320	
Net current assets		31,350
Net assets		190,950
Funded by:		
Owners' capital		45,000
Bank loan		45,000
Profit		100,950
		190,950

'Fixed assets' are those permanent items of long-term value, like land, buildings, equipment and machinery. Of greater day-to-day concern are the 'current assets', which are the ever-changing items, such as stock, debtors and cash, that come and go during trading. 'Current liabilities', like a bank overdraft and debts to suppliers, need to be settled in the near future, usually within 12 months. Subtracting current liabilities from current assets leaves us with our 'net current assets' (or 'net current liabilities' as the case may be). Adding or deducting these to or from our fixed assets produces our overall 'net assets' (or again, possibly, 'net liabilities').

Under or alongside of these figures, we need to show what the firm's activities have been 'funded by'. Here, we might incorporate items such as our own capital, bank loans and profit from our profit and loss account. The total sum should be the same as that for net assets – hence, the 'balance' in the term 'balance sheet'. Again, we might add one or two supplementary comments at the bottom of the statement, just to clarify or expand on entries, as necessary.

Financial requirements

If we are writing this business plan in order to raise finance, we now have to spell out what it is we actually want from the prospective lender. In particular, they will wish to know about:

- the finance needed
- the repayment schedule
- the security available

The finance needed
We must state the amount and type of finance required – whether a mortgage, loan, overdraft or whatever. Following this, we should explain what we will be using it for and when exactly we will need it – to buy a new piece of

equipment in three months' time, for example. It is also sensible to outline how much money we are putting up: most banks will expect us to invest at least as much as we are asking for. They want to see we are committed to the project: if we are not, we cannot expect them to be either.

The repayment schedule
We should also explain how and when we will be able to make repayments on our borrowings. A reputable lender will expect to see a realistic repayment schedule based upon a sensible profit budget, cash-flow forecast and set of projected annual accounts. We must avoid paying back too much too soon, as this could leave us short of much-needed cash reserves later on.

The security available
Although a responsible lender will only provide finance if they can see that repayments can be made from profits, they will still expect us to offer security just in case our business fails and borrowings need to be repaid from other resources. Thus, we need to state what is available, such as equity in the family house or a piece of valuable machinery, and supply evidence of its value and availability. This evidence might be in the form of an estate agent's letter of valuation and proof of ownership.

Summary

We have spent Wednesday looking at how to compile the financial section of our business plan. This involved putting in:

- a profit budget outlining sales, direct costs, overheads and profits, along with explanatory notes and supporting documents
- a cash-flow forecast detailing receipts, payments and balances, plus supporting notes and back-up materials
- annual accounts in the form of a profit and loss account and a balance sheet
- our financial requirements in terms of the finance needed, the proposed repayment schedule and the security available

Adding the appendices

Today, we are going to take a look at our appendices –
those all-important items which verify and enhance the
facts and figures that we put in our commercial and
financial sections. In particular, we need to think about:

- selecting the documents
- preparing the documents
- completing the appendices

Selecting the documents

When we wrote our commercial and financial sections, we
considered those documents which supported our various
comments and details. We now need to read back over
what we stated so that we can pick the right documents for
inclusion in our appendices. Let's consider again:

- our business
- products and services
- our team
- our market
- our finances

Our business
Here, we might want to have copies of annual accounts, the business transfer agent's particulars, an accountant's assessment and any positive newspaper and magazine cuttings about our firm. A map might also be put in to indicate the firm's location and surroundings. With regard to the premises, equipment, machinery and vehicles, we might enclose photographs or scale drawings (or both), the estate agent's details, copies of the freehold deeds or leasehold agreement, the solicitor's comments, a surveyor's report, and copies of planning-permission documents, sales documents and hire-purchase agreements, as relevant.

Products and services
To substantiate and enhance the data given about our goods and services, we could incorporate samples or photographs as appropriate, production schedules, suppliers' price lists, independent test results plus our own price guides, sales literature, and advertising and other promotional materials. We might then put in the same (or abbreviated) information about our rivals' products and services.

Our team

The information that we gave about our team – us, our colleagues and our employees – can be backed up by including curricula vitae, copies of certificates and diplomas, newspaper and magazine features, and copies of either the partnership-agreement or company-formation documents, as relevant. It is important to support any legal papers with a solicitor's letter explaining these. Estimates of professional fees to be incurred for work done externally rather than in-house would be useful additions too.

Our market

To back up the details provided about our customers, competitors and the marketplace, we should think about putting in a map highlighting their respective locations, along with customer sales records, orders and any research findings we have obtained about our customers. For our competitors, we could include materials similar to those used to substantiate facts and figures about our business –

press cuttings, photographs and whatever else is available and relevant. Trade-association reports about the marketplace may be helpful additions as well.

Our finances
Here, it would be a good idea to include proof of any capital available, quotes and estimates of costs and overheads, letters or other documentation from creditors and debtors confirming payment dates, and proof of security that can be put forward as and when loan facilities are provided. Not surprisingly, much of the supporting evidence we might put here will already have been included elsewhere – in customers' sales orders for example.

We have talked a lot about what we should place in our appendices – and rightly so, because they are of crucial importance. It may be beneficial at this point to look at the following master checklist, ticking off those items we intend to incorporate, and perhaps adding others, as relevant to us.

- Annual accounts
- Business transfer/estate agent's particulars
- Accountant's comments
- Newspaper/magazine cuttings about the business, products, team etc.
- Photographs/drawings of premises, equipment, machinery, products etc.
- Copies of freehold deeds/leasehold agreement, plus solicitor's comments
- Surveyor's report
- Copies of planning permission

- Sales documents/hire-purchase agreements
- Product samples
- Production schedules
- Suppliers' price lists
- Independent test results
- Our price guides, sales, advertising and promotional literature
- Data on rival goods and services
- Curricula vitae
- Copies of partnership-agreement/company-formation documents, with solicitor's comments
- Customer-sales records and orders
- Customer-research findings
- Data about competitors
- Trade-association reports
- Proof of capital
- Quotes/estimates of costs and overheads
- Creditors'/debtors' letters
- Proof of security
- What else?

Preparing the documents

Some of our documents may be complex and lengthy in nature, and the reader will need help to find the key information in them. To assist the reader here, let's take a look at what we can do to improve our:

- external documents
- internal documents

External documents
The external documents that we are going to put in our
appendices might come from a wide variety of different
sources, such as these:

• accountants	• European government
• business transfer agents	• media
• estate agents	• solicitors
• chambers of commerce	• suppliers
• colleges and universities	• surveyors
• customers	• trade bodies
• local government	• the Internet
• national government	

Wherever possible, we should try to include the original
documents, unless they are especially valuable or difficult
to replace. The originals are always more believable than
photocopies which have sometimes been used to disguise
altered documentation. Copies of the originals should be
retained for our own records, though.

It is sensible to study each externally supplied item in turn
– sales literature, accounts, press clippings or whatever – to
decide which parts are most relevant to our text and of
interest to the reader. Highlight these areas with a marker
pen to focus the reader's attention on them and away from
other, less relevant information.

Where necessary, be prepared to add an explanatory
comment at the side or bottom of a page – a definition of a
trade expression, an interpretation of a set of figures, or the
date of an unmarked magazine article. We must always
bear in mind who is reading our business plan and amend

our text to suit them – after all, they may not know as much as we do, or indeed anything about our activities at all!

With lengthier items such as a lease or trading accounts for several years, it can be useful to attach a summary of the key facts, for easy reference purposes. This should be set out on a point-by-point basis, and be as brief and concise as possible. Hard facts, rather than opinions, should be put across: the reader can reach an opinion of their own.

Internal documents
Some of the documents that are going into the appendices will come from in-house sources or will be put together by outsiders acting upon our instructions. We might obtain such assorted documents from:

- our own books and records
- the purchasing department
- the production department
- the marketing department
- the administration department
- the finance department
- the personnel department
- photographers
- illustrators
- printers

It is advisable again to put in the originals, even if they are scruffy and perhaps completed in an idiosyncratic manner!

Obviously, a messy set of sales records is not ideal, but at least they are real and believable, and thus far better than those which look false and artificial because they have been rewritten in a new book. And again, we need to highlight key areas, and add explanatory notes and a summary of important facts, if necessary, to make the reading that much easier for our recipient.

There will be materials which we can personally compose specially for this business plan – most notably, curricula vitae, scale drawings of our premises and a summary of customer research findings. Perhaps we surveyed our customers to discover their purchasing habits and opinions. It is sensible to make sure that these documents match the overall, professional image of the rest of the plan, being attractive, easy to understand, realistic and so on. The dos and don'ts of writing a commercial and a financial section apply just as much to the appendices, whenever possible.

Remaining items that may be prepared for us upon our suggestions might include photographs or illustrations (or both) of business premises and goods, sales, advertising and promotional material, and legal documents such as partnership agreements. Evidently, we need to make it absolutely clear what we want and why, but after that we should allow ourselves to be guided by the photographer, illustrator or whomever. After all, we will be paying for their expertise, so we should certainly make the most of it!

Completing the appendices

Now that we have selected and prepared our documents, we must complete the appendices by deciding upon their:

- individual order
- overall position
- general accessibility

Individual order
It is advisable to put the documents in the same order that they were referred to in the commercial and financial sections. Thus, the reader can simply look at each in sequence, referring back to an earlier item as and when required. Avoid the temptation to bring neater and more attractive items to the front and hide other, messy documents at the back, since this will only bewilder and confuse the reader.

Overall position

If we have relatively few documents to include, our appendices can be placed after the commercial and financial sections, all together in the same file. On the other hand, should there be many lengthy or bulky items, it is better to put them in a separate file or folder. Ideally, this should be marked 'Appendices', and will match the main file in order to uphold that all-essential, professional image.

General accessibility

We must provide a list of our appendices somewhere to help the reader who wants to dip in and out as appropriate. If our appendices have been slotted in at the back of the main file, we can detail numbers, titles and pages for the various documents at the bottom of our contents page.

If, however, we have placed our appendices in a second file or folder, we could add something along the lines of, 'Our appendices are in the accompanying file' to the contents page and then affix a list of numbers, titles and pages to the front of this back-up folder. It all makes it that much easier for the reader to find their way around!

Just to add that final touch, we can attach white page-number stickers to the top right corner of each page of the appendices – 'Appendix 6: Estate Agent's Letter: Page 17', 'Appendix 6: Continued: Page 18' and so forth. This enables the reader to find the exact page they want, almost instantly.

Summary

On Thursday, we considered adding appendices to finish our business plan. This meant that we had to:

- select the right documents to support our comments about our business, products and services, team, market and finances
- prepare both external and internal documents so that they could be found and read easily
- complete the appendices by sorting out their individual order, overall position and general accessibility

Submitting a business plan

We now know how to write a business plan, but if it is to be considered a success, we need to have our proposal accepted by the prospective lender, investor or whomever. Therefore, we should focus our attention on submitting our plan properly. This means:

- writing an introductory letter
- delivering the plan
- preparing for a meeting

Writing an introductory letter

It is courteous to send an introductory letter ahead of, or with, a business plan which is going to be studied by someone from outside our organisation, such as a bank manager or would-be investor. As a first point of contact, this letter should convey an impression of smooth professionalism. If we can achieve this, the recipient may be more inclined, or even keen, to read our entire plan. Thus, we need to think carefully about the letter's:

- appearance
- contents
- style

Appearance
If the letter is sent separately in advance of a plan being delivered in person, then we need to begin by considering the envelope. A scruffy, dog-eared one with a misspelt

name or address is not going to put the reader in a favourable mood towards us. We need to choose a top-quality envelope which matches the enclosed paper, rather than a nondescript buff one. The recipient's *correct* name, job title, address and postcode should be printed carefully in the centre of the front of the envelope. A rubber stamp of our firm's name or logo, imprinted at the top left opposite the first-class stamp, adds a classy touch.

Letterheaded and watermarked A4 paper is a must if we want to be taken seriously. Similarly, a typed letter is more formal and professional in appearance than a handwritten one; the text itself has to look neat and easy to read. Generous margins to the top, sides and bottom of the page are helpful, as are short paragraphs of equal length. Tidy and error-free text is just as important: incorrectly spelt or missed-out words make us look careless and amateurish – we should always *rewrite* a letter rather than post it off with any flaws.

Contents

At the top of the page, we should have our letterhead, incorporating the firm's name, address, telephone number, fax number and logo, as relevant. Next, we should type in the date of our letter, putting '17 May 1998' rather than '17th May 1998' or an abbreviation such as '17-5-98' or '17/5/98' which looks sloppy. Under this, we need to detail the reader's name, job title and address. If in *any* doubt, we should check these out – especially their sex, their initials and the precise spelling of their surname. Making a mistake here could irritate or cause offence.

Following on, we must greet the reader by name, rather than by 'Dear Sir' or 'Dear Madam' which conveys the unfortunate impression that this is no more than a circular being sent out to anybody and everyone! Below our greeting of 'Dear Mr di Carlo', 'Dear Ms Thomson' or whatever, we can indicate the subject matter of the letter by putting 'Re:' and a heading which sums up what we are writing about. We could underline this for emphasis if we wish.

Then, we come to the main part of our letter. Typically, we might say who we are and what our business is, if the recipient is likey to be unaware of these points. Moving on, we can then explain the plan itself and say why we have drawn it up and sent it (or why we are *going* to send it) to them. It can be helpful to outline what will happen next – the plan will arrive tomorrow, we will make an appointment to see them in a week's time, or whatever. We need to keep this very brief and to the point. It is an introductory letter, and no more. All of the key information is in the business plan, so we do not have to repeat anything here.

After this, we should end our letter with 'Yours sincerely' or the less formal 'Kind regards' or 'Best regards', as preferred. It is sensible to provide a clear, readable signature rather than one adorned with swirls and embellishments or a rushed and careless squiggle – neither type will impress. Finally, we should add our name and job title, if relevant. 'Enc.' or 'Enclosure' can also be put on a letter if it is being submitted with the business plan itself.

Style

As with the commercial and financial sections of our plan, the letter has to be clear and easy to understand. We must use language to suit the recipient – perhaps technical for a fellow expert, and simplified for a non-specialist. Short words, phrases and sentences tend to be unambiguous and less likely to be misinterpreted. In-house slang, local expressions and personal quirks all increase the possibility of misunderstandings.

It is worth stressing here that the letter *must* be concise. We are simply introducing ourselves and our business plan — *not* trying to give our life history or details of all the ins and outs of the plan. We should therefore check over what we have written, asking ourselves whether the points we have made are relevant to the recipient, and if they are not, we must eliminate them. Then, we need to consider whether we have set out those key points as briefly as we can, watching out for waffle or repetition.

Here is a checklist we can use when writing our letter:

- A top-quality envelope, matching the paper
- The correct name, job title, address and postcode of the recipient on the envelope
- A rubber stamp of our firm's name or logo
- A first-class stamp; it's a first-class proposal!
- Letterheaded and watermarked A4 paper
- Typed, not handwritten; we're professionals!
- Neat and easy-to-read text, using suitable language
- Tidy, error-free text, concise and to the point
- The date
- The reader's name, job title and address – correct again!
- A personal greeting – not 'Dear Sir' or 'Dear Madam'
- The subject matter, 'Re:'
- The main text – who we are, what our business is etc.
- 'Yours sincerely', or similar
- A clear, readable signature
- Our name and job title
- 'Enclosure', if appropriate

It may be useful to look at an example of a good introductory letter:

Gayther Plumbing and Heating Services
76 Thomas Road, Padbury, Sussex ME12 3BB
Tel/Fax: 01724 994312

15 July 1998

Mr B Stone
The Manager
Padbury Bank plc
72 High Street
Padbury
Sussex
ME11 6BT

Dear Mr Stone

Re: 'Brightwell's'

I am a self-employed plumber who wishes to buy the 'Brightwell's' shop at 64 High Street, Padbury.

As I require some financial assistance to purchase and develop this going concern, I am writing to ask if Padbury Bank would consider helping me. A business plan detailing all relevant information is enclosed for your attention.

I have booked an appointment for 11 o'clock on 22 July so that we can discuss this matter in more detail.

I look forward to meeting you.

Yours sincerely

John Gayther

John Gayther

Enclosure

Delivering the plan

Many people spend ages putting together a first-rate
business plan but then fail to deliver it properly. It needs to
reach the recipient in an excellent condition in order to
create that professional image we are seeking to convey.
Just as important, it must arrive *on time*, especially if we are
going to see the bank manager or whomever in a week or
so: they have to be given sufficient time to study the
material in depth, think of questions and draw conclusions
before our meeting. There are three main ways of
delivering our plan:

- by post
- in person
- via an intermediary

By post
Posting the business plan may be a necessity – perhaps we
are trying to raise finance to start a business some distance
from where we live, and are approaching a bank or
building society in that area. If so, we need to make sure
that it is wrapped securely – an apparently obvious point
maybe, but it is not unknown for bank managers to receive
plans through the post which have burst apart during
transit. Not only does this put across a rather shabby
image, but it could also damage the business plan itself,
making it difficult to read. It is also sensible to send it by
registered post so that delivery is guaranteed on a
particular day, and even before a certain time. A registered
delivery has an aura of importance about it too – just what
we want!

Submitting our business plan by post is probably not the ideal method of delivery though – after all, once it is out of our hands, we have lost control, and something could go wrong. Even if nothing goes wrong, we will still be worrying about it for a day or so and making unnecessary (and potentially irritating) 'phone calls to check its safe arrival.

In person
Clearly, the safest way of getting our plan to the person in an excellent condition and on time is to give it to them personally. If we speak to their secretary or whomever in advance, our neat and tidy file or folders can be taken in when we know that they are free and perhaps have an hour or so available to look through our material. Making sure that we ourselves appear equally neat and presentable, we should do no more at this point than introduce ourselves, explain why we are here and hand across the plan. We should end by saying that we look forward to hearing from

them shortly or that we will make (or have made) an appointment to see them in a week's time. This may be wiser, especially if we want a reasonably prompt decision.

Of course, it is not always easy to simply say hello, hand over the business plan and then withdraw as we ought to do at this stage. We may be drawn into a conversation we are ill prepared for, or could be asked questions that we have not yet thought of or thought through. We might not put across the right image, and could even make fools of ourselves.

Via an intermediary
Perhaps it is most sensible to leave our file or folders with an intermediary such as a receptionist, the recipient's secretary or personal assistant, or another responsible member of their staff. This way, we can present it in a professional manner, and know it has arrived and *when* it is likely to be seen by that recipient. Thus, we avoid the problems of packaging, postal damage or loss, and any

potential embarrassment from a face-to-face encounter we have not prepared for fully.

Preparing for a meeting

Ideally, our business plan stands alone, containing all of the commercial and financial information and supporting materials necessary for the recipient to reach a decision – hopefully in our favour! Nevertheless, in most cases we will be expected to attend a meeting to discuss the plan and answer any questions relating to it. By arranging this meeting for a week after the plan has been delivered, we give the recipient a chance to read it, and ourselves sufficient time to prepare for this make-or-break encounter.

When preparing, we should consider three areas in particular:

- our approach
- their questions
- our answers

Our approach
We must make certain that our appearance is appropriate for the meeting. Smart dress – collar, tie and so on – is generally a sensible choice because it acknowledges the importance of the occasion, and shows our respect for the recipient of the business plan. Obviously, it does also depend largely on individual circumstances though. If we know and are on friendly terms with the person, then we can wear whatever would be considered acceptable by them – 'smart but casual', for example. At the same time,

however, we need to feel comfortable. A thick jacket, itchy new top, tight trousers and pinched shoes will feel unpleasant and distract us from the conversation.

How we speak is often regarded as being as important as our appearance. We must ensure that we are heard clearly, achieving this by holding up our head, opening our mouth wide and speaking out in a firm, strong voice. We need to sound confident, sure of our facts and enthusiastic too – if we are not, *they* won't be either. Speaking slowly to emphasise key points can be a good idea as well.

Some thought should be given to our manner during the meeting. We must avoid seeming brash and overconfident, or nervous and servile at the other extreme. Ideally, we should be friendly and sincere, and ready to answer any questions in a polite and positive way. We can help to convey this impression by looking interested throughout, leaning forward and maintaining eye contact and remaining fairly still at all times.

F R I D A Y

Their questions

Not surprisingly, our main worry when we are preparing to meet the bank manager, or whoever has received our business plan, concerns the questions we are likely to be asked. Generally, these questions fall into two broad categories: those arising from the contents of the plan and those relating to the recipient's knowledge of external factors of which we may well be unaware.

Any questions regarding what we put in the commercial and financial sections will probably be asked in order to check facts, clarify vague or confusing text or deal with any omissions. For example, we may not have mentioned a competitor that the recipient is aware of and respects. A good way of anticipating these questions is to let a trusted colleague see the plan and prepare dummy questions for us to answer. It is also sensible to read fully through the business plan just before the meeting to remind ourselves of exactly what we stated and why.

Most of the questions raised will simply seek confirmation of or further information about what we have stated: Why did we put this or that? Is this realistic? What would happen if that payment was not received on time? and so forth. We should be able to handle these comfortably if we know what we are doing, have anticipated the questions in advance and thought of our replies. Unfortunately, there may be one or two questions dealing with issues we do not know about, such as a new competitor who is to start trading soon. These are harder to predict and handle, and so we need to think about how we are going to answer any tricky questions *before* we go into that meeting.

Our answers

When we are asked a question during the meeting, our answer should be an honest one even if it reveals a problem or a lack of knowledge about something. The recipient will not expect this to be a perfect proposal – simply because such a proposal doesn't exist! – and may be happy to help address a difficulty or add to our understanding. They will certainly be more impressed by our honesty than by a waffly response or an obvious lie which would damage our reputation, perhaps irreparably.

If a problem becomes apparent, we should face it, outline our plans for tackling it (or at least coping with it) and then ask for the recipient's opinion. 'What do you think?' flatters the recipient, puts them in a positive mood towards us and may even produce the solution! Should we be unaware of the answer to a particular question, we should say something like, 'I'm sorry, I don't know, but I'll find out and let you know', which shows initiative. Alternatively, we could reply with, 'I'm sorry, I don't know. What information do you have?' if it seems likely that the recipient understands the situation.

Generally, everything we say during this meeting must be brief and to the point – we should adopt the attitude that the recipient's time is valuable and that we do not want to waste any of it. Our comments and responses must be easy to understand too – we should use simple words, sentences and phrases which are suited to the recipient's level of knowledge and understanding of the subject matter.

Naturally enough, what we have to say has to be realistic rather than hopeful – most bank managers have heard it all before and will be distinctly unimpressed by pipe dreams. We should refer when necessary to back-up materials in the appendices. Again, a bank manager wants hard facts, not ifs, buts and maybes.

Summary

Today, we worked on the submission of our plan, and learned how to:

- write an introductory letter with appropriate appearance, contents and style
- deliver the plan by post, in person or, preferably, via an intermediary
- prepare for a meeting by contemplating our approach and anticipating the recipient's questions and our answers

Presenting a business plan

Having submitted our business plan to the bank manager or whomever, we can now move on to *present* it to them. Today we will deal with:

- attending a meeting
- receiving a response
- reviewing our activities

Attending a meeting

If the meeting that we arranged a week or so ago is going ahead, then this is a very good sign: it indicates that the recipient has studied the plan and is in favour of it, or is at least open to persuasion. If they were unimpressed, we would almost certainly have heard from them by now with a rejection letter or 'phone call.

We can view the meeting as involving three distinct stages:

- the beginning
- the middle
- the end

The beginning

Perhaps the most important piece of advice to be given here – and it is not always followed – is to *turn up on time*. There is nothing more likely to annoy the recipient than being kept waiting. If they are, they may be in a rotten mood and we will have less time to discuss our plan. It can be a good idea to make the journey the day before to see how long it takes to get there.

Even if we do not feel it, we should try to appear calm and confident when we walk in, introducing ourselves to the receptionist or whoever is going to announce our arrival to the recipient. We must be prepared to smile, make eye contact and shake hands with the recipient when we come face-to-face with them. Small talk about the weather and our journey may have to be made as well.

When entering the room, we should wait to be shown to our seat rather than sitting down straight away: we may choose the wrong seat, which would be embarrassing for us. We should also decline politely any offer of a drink, sweet or cigarette. These are all potential dangers to us: we could splutter, choke or cough over them, which is distracting and even at times humiliating. It is best to sit there smiling, waiting for the bank manager to talk.

The middle
However long the meeting lasts – perhaps 15 to 30 minutes – most of the time will be taken up by the recipient working through the business plan and asking questions about the commercial section, financial section and so on. Hopefully, we will have anticipated all of the questions and can answer them succinctly, either providing an explanation, promising to find out about something, or asking the recipient what they know about a particular subject.

It is often a sensible idea to take a notebook and pen into the meeting with us. Not only does this give us something to do with our hands which we might otherwise wave about nervously, but it also makes us look professional. We can jot down useful points made by the recipient, add notes about any other work we have to do, and so forth.

Perhaps surprisingly, we should have a copy of the business plan with us too. It is not unknown for bank managers to pull apart a plan and circulate extracts of it to colleagues for their opinions. Sometimes, these are not returned in time for our meeting. If we have full and complete information to hand, then it all helps to make us seem very professional and in control.

The end

Hopefully, a decision will be made towards the end of the meeting, or an indication of the likely decision will at least be given, subject to confirmation by the recipient's superiors. If, however, it is not forthcoming, we should not press for it as this can cause embarrassment or even offence. We should simply allow the recipient to draw the meeting to a conclusion, thank them for seeing us, smile and leave in a pleasant and friendly manner.

After the meeting, we could send a polite letter to the recipient thanking them again for meeting us and stating that we look forward to hearing from them within a certain length of time, typically one to two weeks at most. This is courteous *and* its puts a time limit on their decision. After all, if they are going to reject it, we want to take the plan elsewhere, and soon!

Receiving a response

If a decision has not been announced by the close of our meeting – perhaps because the business plan has to be forwarded to someone else for approval – we would expect to receive either a formal, written response or a more informal 'phone call from the recipient within the following week or so. We then need to deal with the consequences of one of the following:

- rejection
- acceptance

Rejection

A plan which is turned down and returned to us by a
potential source of finance, investment or assistance should
not just be delivered automatically to the next name and
address on our list of prospective lenders or whomever, for
clearly there may be something wrong with it. We should
try to discover *why* it was rejected by studying the letter of
rejection. Or we can 'phone the recipient for an explanation,
if that would be considered acceptable – in most instances,
it will be: after all, we should be entitled to a few minutes'
explanation after all the time and effort we have put into
our plan. However, to obtain a full and honest explanation,
we must maintain our professionalism and not attempt to
persuade them to change their mind. Their decision has
been made, and that's that!

It may be that they think the proposition is not a viable one
or at least is not for them. In either case, we should take
note of their comments, sit down and review carefully our
whole plan and its future prospects. At best, we will
probably need to make some changes and improvements to
it. At worst, it may be best not to proceed at all. Only we
can decide what to do.

Hopefully, we will decide to continue and send the revised business plan elsewhere – to a lender who has a better knowledge of our market, or an investor who is also prepared to become involved in the day-to-day running of the firm, or whomever. Prior to resubmitting it, however, we should replace any pages which have become torn or grubby, remove references included for the last recipient's benefit, and amend outdated text, facts and figures. We need to convince the new recipient that the plan has been written especially for them, and that they are the first person to receive it!

Acceptance

At some stage, and perhaps even the first time around, our proposal will be accepted and we will be offered a loan from a bank, capital from a partner or a leasehold agreement from a landlord. We can now celebrate, albeit briefly, before getting down to business again to expand, diversify, or whatever, and go on to greater success in the future.

Reviewing our activities

We are now going to look back over the week and review our activities day by day. Let's just remind ourselves what we studied each day:

- Sunday   Understanding business plans
- Monday   Making preparatory notes
- Tuesday   Composing the commercial section
- Wednesday   Compiling the financial section
- Thursday   Adding the appendices
- Friday   Submitting a business plan
- Saturday   Presenting a business plan

Sunday
On Sunday, we found out all we needed to know about business plans:

- They usually contain commercial and financial sections, and are supported by appendices which verify and enhance these

- They can be used to raise finance, attract investment, encourage assistance and improve performance
- A successful business plan is well researched, adapted, attractive, understandable, realistic and backed up by independent evidence

Monday

During Monday, we made some preparatory notes by conducting internal research, using external sources and accumulating appropriate information. This meant:

- drawing on our own extensive knowledge
- talking to our colleagues in other departments
- referring to company books and records
- contacting outside individuals and organisations like banks, accountants, solicitors and the media
- approaching other external bodies as diverse as architects, photographers and market research companies
- jotting down notes under the headings 'The business', 'Products and services', 'The team', 'The market', 'Objectives', 'Finance' and 'Appendices'

Tuesday

This was the day that we composed the commercial section of the plan. We included various ingredients:

- the preliminaries – title page, contents page, introduction
- our business – background, location, premises
- products and services – features, selling points
- our team – ourselves, colleagues, employees
- the market – customers, competitors
- our objectives – short-, medium- and long-term

Wednesday

On Wednesday, we compiled the financial section of our business plan. We incorporated:

- a profit budget outlining sales, direct costs, overheads and profits, along with explanatory notes and supporting documents.
- a cash-flow forecast detailing receipts, payments and balances, with supplementary notes and back-up materials
- annual accounts in the form of a profit and loss account and a balance sheet
- our financial requirements, and in particular the finance needed, the repayment schedule and the security available

Thursday

During Thursday, we added appendices to our commercial and financial sections. We selected and prepared documents before completing these appendices. This involved:

- picking the right documents to substantiate the information given about our business, products and services, team, market and finances
- tidying up external documents to make them easier to look at
- producing internal documents which were understandable and simple to study
- putting the documents in the right order and position, and making them accessible

Friday

This was the day that we dealt with submitting a business plan to a recipient. We considered:

- writing an introductory letter, paying special attention to its appearance, contents and style
- delivering the plan, either by post, in person or via an intermediary
- preparing for a meeting with the recipient, with particular emphasis on our approach, their questions and our answers

Saturday

Today, we have had our busiest day. We have looked at how to present a business plan to the recipient, and have contemplated:

- attending a meeting, viewing this in terms of its beginning, middle and end
- receiving a response, discussing how to respond to a rejection or acceptance of our proposal
- all our activities to date, reviewing these on a step-by-step basis

Conclusion

Writing a business plan is a key skill, and to acquire it in a week is a considerable achievement. It is important, however, that we keep working at it, learning from our errors and building on our successes, continually comparing our budgeted with our actual performance, so that we can make constant, ongoing use of this essential business tool, amending and developing it as and when necessary. If – or when – we do this, our organisation will benefit greatly as a result, whether we are using the plan to raise finance, attract investment, encourage assistance or improve performance.